BEYOND
HORIZON
FALL

Maureen Alexandra Fitzpatrick

451

This book is dedicated to the countless beautiful, strong, and resilient families who are engaged in a life or death struggle with a loved one. May you find peace in the knowledge that you are not alone nor to blame. And may you find hope and strength in these words.

I encourage you to write your own thoughts in the space provided at the end of this book.
Try it, you may find a bit of healing there.

CONTENTS

Beyond Horizon FALL

Maureen Alexandra Fitzpatrick

THE BEGINNING: DESPAIR

The day you were born
I cried happy tears

PRIZE

There is no greater love
than the bond between
mother and daughter,
father and son,
at least for awhile.
I never knew the devil
had a bond stronger,
a hypnotic prize just for
you.
And so a new
relationship began,
A blossoming love,
becoming all consuming,
And I was cast aside.

SAFETY

This little child with hair
of gold,
so full of life, story
untold.
Her pain misunderstood,
confusing her mom,
lost in the abyss,
walls too high to climb.

Find my hand child,
I need saving too.

*They'll say the devil
made you do it;
I'd have to agree*

THE DEVIL'S DANCE

A rabid dance

Between mother and child

Daughter and drug

Writhing
Swirling
Twisting

Violent efforts to shake

The devil's music

From her soul

Where are you my child?
Please
Return to me

A Break

The enormity of this
world in which I sleep
Overwhelms me

Chirping crickets and
foraging bears
Intrigue me

Gentle breeze
Rustling leaves
Sooth me

Thoughts of you alone
Somewhere
Terrify me

Goodnight, my love
I miss you

CHAINS

Chains of burden,
shame, and guilt
Strapped to her chest
Trudging up hill

There she climbs a drug
filled cliff
Her body weary, in need
of rest

Take the ropes and hold
on tight
I'll pull you in, make it
alright

I heard you crying somewhere

TODAY

Today is hard.
I've no idea where you
are, why you left; and
you have no idea that
your actions are causing
my spirit to shatter, my
soul to die, my hope to
diminish and my life to
crumble.
How dare you!

Just for a moment
I close my eyes and let
sleep wash over me.
I pray sometimes that I
don't wake up.

THE FEAST

Devil's keeper walking,
Prince of Darkness
stalking, machetes in
their mitts.
Duck, my love.
Their life is nourished by
your fear, and they will
steal extra rations if you
let them.
Steer them away from
your smorgasbord, for
they seek shelter under
gray aura. And they will wait,
and stalk, and
pounce ravenously,
anxious to destroy your
strength with their
weapons, desperate to
drink your blood until
you die a quiet, woeful
death. Run to me, let me
help. I'm wearing steel
toed boots and will kick them
hard in the shins.
Then maybe, just maybe,
you might find a bit of
peace

HOWLING WIND

Allow me to follow your
woeful song.
Screeching wind bristles at
my ears.

I see her there, head
nodding, chin glistening,
spittle
dribbling.

I'm scared.
I didn't think eyes could roll
back any further.

She scratches.
Scabs of yesterday become
scars of tomorrow; the
picking never ceases.

Locked behind the bathroom
door, one hour, two hours,
three hours, till I bust the
damn thing down, only to sit
her next to me and watch her
head fall to dented Formica.
Again, the hospitals won't
keep her. They never do.
What the hell???

Dammit. The sound of the
howling wind refuses to
cease.

I'm only a little glad you're home. Life is easier when I don't have to watch you die.

BULLSHIT

Sometimes I wonder where
I am, if I'm real, if there really
is a shiny blue sky above
me. So often it feels like a
dream, an impossibility to feel
something other than grief,
a futility to believe in life and
hope and pretty pink flowers.
I look around and I see it, but
all I feel is the evil fertilizing
our kids, the chemical bullshit
masquerading as peace.

THE GAME

Dangle my heart over a cliff;
you may as well set it adrift,
amongst the septic souls
with whom you allow, to steal
your soul after you took a
vow,
To stay away!
To push away!
the very devil that stole your
life,
and set me afloat in a world
of strife,
of hopelessness and torrid
pain,
and now I may never see you
again.
You've lost yourself to the
monster of drugs,
and I've lost myself to the
push and shove,
of playing my cards to help
you survive.
I've lost the game,
it won you, but I've died.

The Crown

She slumps in a crack house
Dead eyes cast down
Riches stolen from loved
ones
Buy a rat feces crown
Lonely, despondent, filthy and
sick, open sores ooze lost
hope, danger lurks with each
trick
Her life was once vibrant
Now I'm afraid death might
win
My daughter's a stranger,
Fuck heroin!

Allow me to lead you to greener
pasture,
Come,
take my hand

BLACK HOLE

And finally the day came,
Dead pall falls
Covering hope's mercy
With doubt's midnight hell,
A black hole epiphany,
A remembrance revisited.

TROPHIES

Trying to sleep during a
waking nightmare is fun,
A pessimistic game of who
will win: the monstrous pain
or slumber?
I saw pain's shelves the other
day
filled to the brim with
trophies.

BOOM

What if the world ended, a
big boom explosion,
rupturing deities, detonating
personal assumption,
not from a nuke or ISIS,
but from the malevolent
energy of our souls,
disconnected through distrust
and hurt, envy and sadness?
What if all that was left was
suspended in time? A spiritual
ghost of what could have
been, had we not tossed
personal filth towards the
prosperity of others. Imagine
if all that was left was nothing.
Love. Just love.

BRICKS

The first brick went up.

"I refuse to go to school
today."

The second brick went up.

"I don't have to listen to you!"

The third brick went up.

"I hope you fucking die!"

The fourth brick went up.

"Your daughter seems fine.
We are sending her home
from the ER."

The fifth brick went up.

"She's your problem, lady!"

The sixth brick went up.

"Please come home and help
me with her now!!"

The seventh brick went up.

"This is CBS news reporting a missing girl."

The eighth brick went up.

"My daughter threw her body though my picture window. I want her arrested!"

The ninth brick went up.

"Your child is being arrested for burglary."

The tenth brick went up.

"HIPAA laws allow her to leave this hospital if she chooses."
The eleventh brick went up.

"But she's only 16, and she's sick!!"

The twelfth brick went up.

"Lady, I can't put her in rehab if she doesn't want to go. I don't care if you're her mother."

The last brick went up.

"My kid would never do that.
Where are her parents?"

The truth is, I was here all
along, fighting for my child
from behind this massive
brick wall

*Do you know I've heard people
say we should have been better
parents? Fuck them. How do
explain addiction to those with
their heads buried in sand?*

MAYBE

I've dreams still, heroin's
ugly face chasing you, razor
teethed fear biting down on
you, on me.
The beginning: Teenaged
awkward loneliness, bat-
whacked self esteem,
Mt. St. Helen's combustible
anger combining, erupting,
pouring forth tear filled
lava, trapping your beauty
underneath, to suffocate,
drown, in the hot turmoil of an
executioner's plan.
For heroin only has one
goal dear, to kill; to smile as
a parent buries their very
soul along with their child,
joining thousands of other
varsity letter holders, high
school band leaders, softball
pitchers, and beautiful geeks
deep inside maggot filled,
body rotting earth.....eternally.
If only you knew your worth.
If only I had held you more.
If only every God forsaken
drug dealer could step into
a parent's nightmare for
even a few seconds and
truly feel the torturous,
helpless, grinding, rip your
heart out raw, no anesthesia,

unbearable dagger of that
five buck devil. If only....
Then maybe, just maybe
you'd be ok.

SOLACE

I think back at times

And my body becomes

a vibrating base

Pouring dark

reverberations

deep into my soul

Causing me to stop

breathing

Inviting panic in

as the slow, low pitched

music plays

the Bogey Man's theme

song

And I pray for release

Solace

More time in between

To forget

To forgive

To live

To love

*Faith doesn't sleep with me
anymore. Distrust and anger do.
Faith is for those who believe in
magic. I prefer to believe in you.*

FAITH?

They tell me to believe,
to find faith, as if it were a
simple child's bouncy ball lost
under thick brush.
"How can you live without
faith?" they ask.
I ask, "How can I live with
it?" You see, I had it once,
at least a miniscule dose,
when I prayed for healing
from a summer's cold or
stomach cramps. But I knew
they'd heal anyway, with or
without religion. But when
I put my faith in Him when
I needed it most, comfort
and relief from the mental
storm raging within you, my
child, I found none. Night
after night the storm raged,
rearing its ugly head more
vehemently each episode,
and the little faith I had, fell
to the tempest. Yes, it is
easier to live without God, for
then the disillusionment and
abandonment don't hurt quite
so much. No expectations....
no disappointment.

I wish you'd open the bathroom door.
I can't stand the thought of breaking down another door, yet I can't stand the thought of not.

I'VE NO RIGHTS

I thought you'd be smarter
with hiding it. I guess you're
now at the point you just
don't care. There are tinfoil
pieces and burnt spoons
everywhere; there are
shoelaces and little baggies
all over the house. With all
this evidence and your rolled
back eyes and needle marks,
I still can't get you into rehab
BECAUSE YOU REFUSE.
Where are my parental
rights?

HEROIN'S NIGHTMARE

A Poem by Her

"Ping"
The elevator glides open
"Wait," I think to myself.
"This can't be right." I step
out into total darkness,
the sound of my footsteps
all that echoes through
the still. I look around,
bewildered, confused, but
curious. Suddenly there's
a flickering of light in the
distance. I'm captivated.
It's enchanting. A sense of
glory and warmth pour over
me as I make my way to
its beauty. The darkness is
now just background noise.
The simplicity of the light
casts away the terrors of
the night. I start running, my
excitement getting the best of
my will. Running, running, run!
Something is wrong. What is
taking so long? Why haven't I
reached my flame? Panic sets
in. The beauty of the light
fades, and the more I run, the
further it is. The knots in my
chest are churning. The flame
is dimming and the heat is
rising.

Then...blackness. Whoosh!! I know I am not alone. I feel the demon's breath. Choking on ash, I try to catch my breath, trying to catch my thoughts as they dash by hundreds of miles per hour. My breath shortens, each attempt to breathe stopped by the knots in my stomach until they are held captive for good. The room starts spinning, shaking, spiraling down.
Slam!
I sit up in a haze, the black now grey. All that is light and all that is dark become one. No emotion, no concern, just wandering.

You surprise me with your intelligence.
Don't give it to the demons. Use it for good.

CRAZY ME

I'm crouching like the

girl in the crazy movies,

in a corner, head down,

shaking, crying,

screaming, scared I

might stay here forever.

It's the only place I feel

safe today.

Carry me Lord as you carry her
too
But if we get too heavy
Please lay me down and just
carry her

Sad Life

Phone confiscated
Money lost
Car towed
Overload

Boyfriend booked
Purse stolen
Key inside
Pimp a ride

No entrance
All alone
Standing small
Gonna fall

Sad soul
Yes, my dear
Drugs suck
I give a fuck

Lost mind
Too bad
You did this
You took the risk

Beg a pass
For the bus
Grab a cup
Toughen up

Then check into
Rehab please
Before you die
And make me cry

*Are you thinking today that
you'd finally like to get better?
Or will you once again tell
me you like living in the flea
bag motel, with a drugged up
stranger, pissy shit mattress, and
rotten smelly God knows what?*

RESCUE ME

I awaken again to
nothingness,
to invisibleness,
the lonely echo of my own
breathing,
pounding me,
raping me,
crushing me
under the weight of phantom
woe,
every thrust pushing me
further and deeper
into restless hell.
And as the new day breaks,
I hear the love songs of birds,
and I reach out my hand
offering my soul
to the beauty outside my
barren chamber,
and I pray
that someone, somewhere,
feels my hungry plea for
respite,
and will rescue me
from this infertile assault
and pull me safely into the
comfort of their arms

Your brother vomited in my car today. You know, because we raced outside to escape your drug fueled violence. I love you, child, but this can't go on.

HOPE

We murmur of forever

Of life lived fully

Dancing on the precipice of
now and then

Soon and never

Waltzing back and forth

Here and there

Singing happy songs as we
tumble on black leather

Giggling

Unsure but not unaware

That this time is precious

Rare

And that whispered hopes
and cha chas

Give lyrical context

To the meaning of family

The swirls are the worst
The unsteady shaky whirling
that rarely ceases
They say it's anxiety,
But I know it's fear

Walking Away

She asked me to die today.

"Fuck you, fuck you, die!"

-Because I love her and can't
help her anymore, until she
helps herself-

My beautiful princess,
waiting in her dungeon to be
rescued.

But I choose to turn away,

And walk towards the pretty
fields of green.

Fuck me
Fuck me

I think I have died

HITHERLAND

Hitherland they wail

Empty trumpets

Desperate sounds

They sing in solitary

Confinement

Theirs alone

If I keep up this crying
We will all die together
In a river of tears

FAIRY TALE FAITH

Splintery wooden prayers
unanswered,
I was down on my knees for
you, Lord.
Where the hell were you?
I cried tears I never knew I
had,
Shiny-pew church dreams
shattered as you turned your
back on my pain, on hers.
Good Lord, God.
Who and where are you?
Do you exist, or is the fairy
tale faith I had just that,

a fairy tale?

BEAST

Somewhere in the night
lives the beast of prey,
feeding on the last vibrant
droplets of dreams from
the downtrodden, his fangs
carefully poised and ready
to pounce when another
leaden step stumbles, falls.
His hunger, an angry monster
of empty promise, a barren
chamber of acidic need, will
follow you into the path of
gory uncertainty, a place to
maim, a place to kill.
The gloom has come, hope
is now buried beneath
treacherous longing. Fear
is your new friend, a gentle
caress of warning. Heed her.
Run, baby, run.

EMPTY

Hollow echoes of despair
toss silent sounds of futility
'round and 'round and 'round.

It's empty in there.

Black nihility filled with
spacious nothingness
surrounds in chill's forlorn
grip. Welcome to the death of
something that was.

It's empty in there.

Like the prosperity of Gospel
or the starving gullet of lone
Siberian lemmings,

It's empty in there.

Such is my heart:
Bared, naked, and void of
feeling.
That's what the blue bag
does to a mom.
Get well, so I don't have to
stay......

empty in there.

*I often wonder about
the dog shows. I thought
allowing you to travel would do
you good, allow you to find a bit
of peace in your cyclonic mind.
Maybe I was wrong.*

DECEIT

Medals and honors and fancy
wins

I see dogs, snarling

They wear deceit in their
coats and manipulation in
their tails

Claws scratch the shiny
surfaces

You smile as you prance with
them

They smile as they grant you
another victory

And as they sniff, so do you.

GODS

Matted, curly hair gods walk
around town.
How I sometimes pray
murder were legal.
They float above the
sidewalks
out on bail again.
And they flaunt their power,
their Houdini magic,
free again from iron bars,
"Smile people. We are back.
Nothing can get us. Lol, lol,
lol! "
A bullet would.
But there'd be no Houdini
breaks for me.
Somehow those matted, curly
headed gods always win.
I hate them.

FUNERAL

Your funeral has happened
Words of wisdom have been
spoken to the crowd
Tears have been cried and
songs sung
They played your favorite
song
We ate your favorite food
We shared your favorite
stories
And we cursed the drugs that
took your life
Yes, you are still here
But I've already been to your
funeral.

SOMEONE

Jackass, scumbag

or is he?

I love you.

Someone must love him.

But why is he sitting in the
convenience store parking lot
in his rusted Chevy
waiting for you?

Jackass, scumbag

I followed you.

I caught him.

Put my Lincoln bumper
against his dilapidated junker.

Told him to get the fuck out of
town, while praying a bullet
didn't cut my thoughts.

Low life loser

He had to be 40.

I should have called the
cops.

Instead I played vigilante.

It kind of felt good.

I lived through it.

I hope he learned from it.

Lowlife, scum

THE INVADER

It's a wonder this pain doesn't
kill, the way the tired ego
cries with each dagger,
defeated,
knotty black joylessness alive
with fury,
a woman held hostage,
scratching deep within,
clawing, clawing, clawing her
way out. Tonight I'll open my
window,
then my mouth,
hopeful that she will disgorge
herself through the corroded
cavities of my being, leaving
a bitter aftertaste I can gargle
away from my soul

B12

The dark pall suffocates.
Its evil essence stalls,
purposely, intent on
squeezing the last ounce of
air from my lungs.
I'm ready for a brawl, a last
fucking go; a test of my b12.
Broken dreams are my
strength.
I think of all I've given self-
lessly. And in this moment
I wish I'd been more selfish.
For in the end it doesn't
matter.
"Fuck you," it mocks.
"Yes, fuck me," I answer.
At least we agree on that.

*Putrid vomit expels itself from
the confines of my pith.
Rancid agony fills the air, it
smells,
I hurt.
Where the hell are you?*

Days Like This

I hate when the punishable
thunder rumbles from afar,
damning my soul, tearing
chasms into the very core of
my being, spilling the blood
I had so carefully saved for
a day my heart would truly
need to bleed for you.
Yes, I'm nothing now but a
casperous shell wishing these
past eight hours go stuff
themselves.
Hard.
My mama forgot to tell me
there'd be days like this.

SOS

What am I really searching for
when the veil of uncertainty,
waltzes clumsily before me?
When one day I'm sure, then
at the next harbor, doubtful?
Which lighthouse will guide
me home from stormy turmoil,
to grant me peace, to gift me
love's precious shelter, to
allow me to once again feel
the simple silken sand as it
cascades gently between
my toes? To which beacon of
strength shall I crawl to save
myself from drowning?

REFUSE

Night comes too early
to those who wish for light.
Selfish notions squeeze away
self indulgent thoughts of
misery's contentment.
Frayed chord circles life's
uncertainty, dangling like a
noose around willful breaths.
Pessimistic thoughts will be
hung tonight and uncertainty
left in the gallows.
For though night will surely
come,
refuse to let the darkness
win,
refuse to bow to madness.

Door slams in stunned face
drafting whiffs of Marlboros
She thinks me a pest

Soldiers

Sometimes there are just too
many pressures advancing,
tin soldiers armed with
grenades.
"Ready, aim. Fire," they yell.
Their taunts and blasts
fire deep into the core,
threatening to shake any bit
of peace currently contained.
There's always one bomb
that stings like hell,
burning into self's center and
tearing up the soul.
Nothing hurts more than
unexpected explosions in
carefully guarded hearts.

Corpse

Earthy marrow coats paper
thin epidermis.
Minuscule droppings mix with
the decaying skin.
I'm six feet under
listening to the pounding rain
above,
hoping for a dribble,
a bit of liquid life.
But the only life I feel is the
maggots making love to the
decaying corpse called me.

I hate jagged edges.
They cut.
I hate drugs.
They have jagged edges.

I DON'T LIKE HIM

Your friend Stefan was surely
swell.
Love the guy.
Such a beautiful and giving
soul to introduce you to
drugs,
such a trusting and loyal
friend to stay by your
side during your arrests
and incarcerations and
disappearances and near
overdoses.
Yes, Stefan is such a loyal
friend. For who else would be
there after all those trials to
give you a little more of this
or that to get you through.
Such a beautiful gift.
Such a beautiful giver.
Ugh.

HIS NAME IS DRUG

I've been swindles by the
drug too. Not in the way you
have. You see, I never took
him, never would think about
taking him, but he still fooled
me. He made me believe
your lies so many times I can't
count. He led me into naivety,
when I should have known
better. He shook me down for
fear of his violence so much,
that I retreated rather than
stood. He held me hostage,
when I should have been
strong.
He almost killed me
and my family,
and I almost let him.
I always thought I was strong.
Apparently, I'm not.

PANIC AT MY DISCO

I feel the cascading tears,
liquid marbles tracing,
following the labyrinth of 206
marrowed bones, paths of
strength.
They say jittery skeletons
are not real. They live only
in the dark crevices of the
desperate underworld,
aching to be realized. But I
see them.
I feel them.
I am them.
I hang desperate, noosed and
gasping for air.

Rattle, rattle, roll, gasp!

What is that sound but the
dark destitution of loneliness,
an anxiety filled display of
unselfish talent?
Percussion at its finest.
Jittery bones jitter and quake.
Drum roll please!

Tum, tum, tum!

Beautiful music of a fearful
soul.
Devil's delight.
Let's dance with our thorns
upon our head, spirit half

dead.
Lonely symphony crying,
spirit of one dying.
Don't tell me it's all in my
head. Just take a look.
You will see my dread.
Panic lives, panic sings.

Rattle, rattle, roll.

*Had I known this life would have
me carry the tormented anchor
of a thousand suffering souls, I
might have taken a detour.*

Rain

And so it rains...
Dripping drops of muddy
grey,
falling razor sharp through
the smoky mists of sorrow,
sharp and cutting into her
brave skin,
emitting wafts of rancid iron
and wailing crimson,
tides of an unfair world.

She stands there naked,
exposed, and proud,
a stalwart sacrificial lamb,
beautifully tragic,
a lone creature amongst
greedy dealers,
giving her last shards of
heartfelt fortitude to the wind.
The rain whips.
The rain wallops.
And so she bleeds.
Good God, have mercy.

RIVER

I'll cry a thousand tears
from the lonesome confines
of my head,
Create the perfect river,
I'll go floating there instead.
I'll look for someone there
to glide down salty and free,
Holding hands together,
I hope it's you and me.

*Can't you just go on a heroin
diet? Just don't use it. I'll do
it with you, but I'll give up
chocolate. I promise. Let's do
this together.*

LOLLIPOPS

Sometimes in life everything
sucks

You try to be what
everyone wants

but still everything sucks

You give 10000% of your soul

but still everything sucks

Give me a thousand
popsicles and ten thousand
lollipops

I'll make it real

I'll make sure

everything sucks

CANNON

I just realized,
I am a loose cannon.
Maybe that's better than that
stiff board part of me.
Perhaps I will use the cannon
to break the board,
to make a tent where I
can meditate and relax so
my cannon doesn't fire so
impulsively again.
Hmm, there's an idea.

HOPE'S DEATH

Perhaps it's a blessing.
Hope's last will was written
up in winter news, a clear
indication that she had at
last died. Never again will
the August flame of a perfect
soul shine down upon her
innocence, allowing a little bit
of light to reach her broken
heart, or to set her amber
tresses aglow. As eulogies
go, it was a good one, an
outline of once was, including
her faith in yesteryear's
promise and her triumphs
so many years ago over the
evil tug of pessimism. Yes,
hope has died. The constant
barrage of words used as
ammunition, shot in tiny
bursts into her soul, chipping
away at whatever health she
could hold onto, finally killing
her. The disease of a self
loathing, self centered world
tore the last bits of her in
two, leaving a path of bloody
entrails, a final gift to the filthy
varmint of the world, oh so
happy to feast once more.
Hope,
may she finally rest in peace.

Your dad is strong, but your
friend heroin is killing him,
killing us.
Our hands are being torn apart,
our hearts barely holding onto
this tether of despair.

HELL

Just how far down is hell,

six feet or sixty million?

Human furnace,

wafts of ribs barbecued

in solidarity or maybe

solitary, had the deeds

pursued living

outweighed in

repugnance those of

another. And if I should

die before I wake and

head to hell my soul to

take, I wish to find an

inglenook, sixty million

feet down, to hide for

just a moment, before

the fiery pit of Abaddon

makes me scream for

mercy as my tears of rue

and regret dance

upward in pretty swirls,

steamy ribbons of death,

to bless the living with

my mournful gift, my

debt of compunction, a

chilly morning fog.

MAKE ME A TREE AGAIN

This paper, my heart, two
halves, ink black

This life, this love,
this drug, so smug

My words, her words, these
fights, our poem

Then rip, then tear,
my paper, her hair

My words, they fall,
get trampled, then stall

In mud, my sonnet
Her rage, her comet

My life, this page,
Debris, thrown away

I can't reach her, she left
I'm once again, bereft

This paper, this poem our
song, long gone
I wish I were once again a
tree

*I was working at a new job when
you called,
threatening to kill yourself.
I started to panic in a room full
of sixth graders.
I had to run home from that new
job repeatedly. I'm surprised
they didn't send me packing.*

SHAKY

I still get shaky.
A lot.
When I type or drive.
I might even get heart
palpitations and a light head.
The reaction is always the
same,
panic in one form or another,
over a trip to a restaurant,
or a harp lesson,
or a baseball game.
"Boo, I'm still here!" panic
tells me.
I had hoped him gone.
But he rides along in the car,
sneaks into my purse, follows
me to the shower,
wants to take over my
shadow, I believe.
That fear,
that unbelievable emotion of
dread,
that haunting overflow of
hopelessness is here sitting
next to me.
Still.
I wish I could just swat him
away.

Threads of intestine, knots of gore, tie me up daily. Rotten brain pleas don't help. When a soul starts to die, begging help from a sick body falls on deaf ears.

BESEECH

I beseech thee, oh heart, to
allow me a moment's peace,
to banter with my restless
brain,
to implore it to forget love's
dying hold.
Allow me a restful slumber
curled up with my grandma's
quilt,
fluffy socks and humming
rain,
to rock my aching soul gently
away from incessant thoughts
of her dying grace,
her joyless song.

RESURRECTION

Last week the knots in my
stomach threatened to break
and bleed me out, until my
corpse descended gracefully
over the crumbed up
linoleum of the kitchen floor.
And yes, yesterday was
better, thanks to an ongoing
dizzy spell warping my mind,
and a gaggle of silly teens
running about,
but today hurts once more;
tear producing, heart
shattering, tummy spasming
bad.
Though if my hollow corpse
could fall and rise once
already, perhaps it's not out
of divine resurrections.

Our Cups Runneth Over

God only gives us what we
can handle. It's the nice
people's way of saying, we've
no choice but to deal with
the cards we've been dealt.
Short of suicide, truly what
choice do we have? Who
decides our capacity for
anything, our ability to fill up
our stress cups before they
runneth over? Or do we have
multiple stress cups? Maybe
a shot glass for work shit and
a tumbler for kid shit, green,
with middle fingers pointing
towards the heavens. We've
each a capacity to do more
than we've ever imagined.
In simplest form, it's shown
with the millions of people
who awaken each day and
head, robotic like, to jobs
that slowly tear them apart;
a big, green cup chewing
machine, creating cracks,
and painting wear, but never
allowing the true measure
of our capacity to reach its
rim. Maybe the bits of stress
that leak through the fissures
grant us more time before

we overflow, before we
jump off that bridge, use that
gun, or twist from the pain
of madness. But then there
are the family problems, the
other problems. I can imagine
internal boxes slowly being
filled. Dad and Mom don't
get along, Sarah uses drugs,
Joey has cancer, Suzy is a
klepto, Daddy fooled around.
How much can one person
take? How many tons of
Xanax and Paxil and Zoloft
will be dispensed? Just dump
it in the damned water; we all
need it. How many gyms will
gain memberships with those
looking to de-stress, only to
lose them because people
are too stressed to get there?
Yes, we all have our little
boxes, our shot glasses, our
green, fuck you tumblers
within. But look around.
I see too many of them
overflowing, their stench and
poison reaching those left
still half full. God didn't give
everyone the ability to handle
their portion of difficulty.
Unfortunately.

FEELINGS

Carefully manicured feelings
tumble down,
and the big bad queen found
me hiding.
Not sure why I feel the need
to run,
to shroud myself from
something.
I feel like I'm holding the
poison apple and I'm
supposed to take a bite.

*Bitterness and anger continue to
swell in tidal waves.
Bring a wave of peace soon, so
I'm not left wondering when I will
be washed away for good.*

REALLY MILEY?

I see Miley sing of partying
with Mollies.
What's she thinking; that it's
safe? Harmless? Fun jollies?

Free speech some might
say, but I say bullshit to that.
She's not just singing, she's
luring others, that brat.

Has she seen what these
drugs have done
to families like mine? Taken
bright solid minds and blown
them up fine?

Not to mention the pain put
on my child's siblings and me,
and the thousands of dollars
spent to set her mind free.

The violent episodes when
drugs fueled her rage,
the cops, the neighbors, and
siblings her stage.

Gave me PTSD, yes, it's true
from that shit.
What the drugs did to her, to
me harder they hit.
For those of you thinking just
once might be fun,
that's all it takes, my advice is
to run.

Your skin will scab over.
Your soul will be bare.
You will end up dead. Who
can visit you there?

Don't think for a second, "It
will not be me."
The honest truth is,
neither did she.

Her love for her family has
been replaced,
by a false love for drugs,
yes, pills took our place.

Straight A student, star
pitcher she was,
Until her life went awry, once
she got her buzz.

Now she's missing
somewhere, and she's up to
bad strife.
And I'm hoping this message
can help save your life.

*I'm feeling broken like shattered
glass. Please make the glue to
fix it invisible.
I don't want more scars*

WINE FOG

By another daughter, her sibling,
Mary Kate

Wine fogged memories
become so clear.

I taste copper in my mouth
and realize it is blood from
biting my tongue for so long.

I remember, God, I remember.

And I sob because I don't
want to.

It's so easy to forget,
to pretend to forget, bottle
up my tears and sell them as
witch's potion,
Put a label on and call
it "Passive aggressive
heartbreak."

I loved you, and you broke
me.
And through awkward phone
calls and forced laughs we
try to come back, because it
hurts even more to imagine
this pain as permanent.

Your siblings love you, they just can't show it right now. Someday they will. A child's heart breaks like the fragile, crystal spun sugar of fairies. Get better and show them your true self. Then all that sweet sugar will come your way.

CRYSTALS

*Another by Mary Kate, my
daughter, her sibling*

There is no easy way to
describe the exact way a
heart can break. Mine broke
slowly, so much that I didn't
even notice, so much beyond
repair that I still haven't
figured out quite how to fix
it. I think it was the first time
I saw Mom cry, how broken
you'd made her;
that was the first shard of
glass that cut me, though
there were so many scattered
across the floor from your
violent rage. It felt like they
were embedded beneath my
skin, absorbed by my blood,
until I could not remember
how it felt to be alive without
constant pain flowing within
me.
I can still feel the shards,
though you've tried to clean
them up. Year after year
you get better at sweeping
them under the rug; I guess
you forget the ones I've
swallowed, the sadness
that still lives within me. My
heart broke in small ways:
everyday that I could not fix

you, everyday that you lost
yourself in an even deeper
pain
that none of us could
understand. I do not pretend
to forgive you for all you've
done, but I will say this: In
certain lights, broken glass
can look like crystals, and
sometimes, when you look
long enough they sparkle like
God.

THAI FOOD

Another by Miss Mary Kate

We talk over exotic spices
and foreign languages until
the room is as warm and
comforting as the bottle of
Merlot on the table. Your
wine stained lips, so sweet,
speak of things so terrible
that you've endured, and I try
not to cry because I know it
embarrasses you. You tell me
of love turning to ashen dust
in your hands and wayward
children led astray by evils
we don't understand,
of rose tinted dreams
dissipating under the
merciless tide of life, and of
prayers unanswered by some
kind of cruel God.
As you speak your eyes
replay the horrors of a tragic
past, and I can feel the pain
as they shield behind blue
armor the same color as the
skies of a heaven you don't
believe in anymore. I fail in
the attempt to stifle my tears,
because I remember thinking
I had never seen a woman
more beautiful and broken,
that nothing happens for a
reason, because it would be

some kind of a fucked up
God to allow the very flesh
and blood of a woman to
damage her so completely.
Perhaps it is some kind of
blood sacrifice needed, a
pagan God of such, thirsty for
the blood of the innocent.
I do not understand why
bad things happen to good
people and why such good
intentions pave the road to
hell. All I know is that you are
the most wonderful woman I
have ever met, and on nights
when there is static stillness
and I lay my head across your
lap, I cannot feel your jagged
edges, only the soft sound of
constant love.

Love is funny.
We are supposed to love
unconditionally. I suppose I do,
however, when the devil attacks,
I second guess that "given."

BAD MAPS

I don't know what you are
thinking
I don't understand how you
got there
I just know you must be truly
hurting
In excruciating pain for which
any salve I've tried to apply
failed. You are lost without
direction. The maps I've
thrown you must be wrong.
For you are still not home.
The turmoil and distorted
thinking have traveled from
you to me.
I'm feeling it.
I'm empty, twisted inside.
What can I do to save you?
Can I save you? Can you
somehow feel my words?
Somewhere? They are trying
to lead you home.

SILENCE

Frank discussions over
broken plates and piece meal
lives,

"Is she badly designed?"

"No she's God's child too, our
child."

"What God?" I ask.

"Ask him for strength. That's
what he gives, not miracle
fixes."

My husband the accountant,
pfftt,
what would he know of God?

Who here on earth has seen
God, met him, talked with him
personally?

"But if he's all that,
why can't he perform
miracles? I hear he's
supposed to. I've prayed," I
say.

"Look, I don't profess to have
all the answers; talk to a
minister."

I forgo that idea and instead,
take it back to the top.

"God, I ask," Where are you
when I need you? "

Silence

Do moms and daughters,
fathers and sons,
speak different languages? Yes
and yes

DADDY'S GIRL

*A beautiful try at a poem by
her dad*

Sweet first child, so filled with
spunk,

What an athlete you were,
catching balls like a pro as a
toddler!

Your gifts so plentiful: soccer,
softball, A1 pitcher, basketball,
dog handler, stepdancer, oh
what fun we had! After all, I
am your dad.

Then came the pain. You
thought you were fat,
developed eating issues,
friend issues, life issues. You
rode the totem pole down
to the bottom and as you
slipped down, a monster
grew.

Deadly friends, drugs,
cursing, stealing, fighting,
hitting. You hated me. Wished
me dead.

Our family was good. What
happened?
Soon you were kicked out,
cops came repeatedly; you

went missing for weeks. I died inside wondering about your safety. How could I parent the others, be a good husband?
I couldn't. I tried.

The stress took its toll. When I couldn't sleep night after night, wondering if you were dead or alive, when my anxiety reached its peak, when I felt the shame, guilt, stress, sadness every day, I wondered if I'd get through, we'd get through.

But the light has peaked around the clouds. The rays are beginning to shine. You are alive, you have begun anew, you are making positive choices, you are living.
And you are forgiven and loved.

To truly see
To truly feel
Take some steps up a
mountainside,
Alone

THE NEXT CHAPTER: HOPE AND LIFE

*I'll carry your heart with me in
my backpack,
and as I wander and walk,
I'll feel your love tickling my
spine.*

Peace

To achieve true serenity

Cast away rage

Fling away loathing

Release sadness

Cull boredom

Reel in chocolate

ADVERSITY

Adversity is like a glacier.
It's cold, hard to climb over,
and knocks you back to the
bottom when you get close to
the top.
Take out your ax, and put on
your crampons. Don't let a
hunk-a-frozen water win.

Understanding a teenager is like
understanding quantum physics.
You just don't.

I BELIEVE IN YOU

Monster face fear
The doubt explodes
Too much to bear
On overload
Just take today
And make it shine
Then think of joy
You will be fine

Rejoice in your strength
Smile at the breeze
Breathe in fresh grass
A pollen fresh sneeze
Hold true to yourself
Let fear fall away
You've got this, my girl
In life you will stay

Take a lesson from your dog
Don't worry, be happy

BREAK FREE

When you feel your back
against the wall,

Try to appreciate the cool
wood on your back and the
smooth feel of the panel,

Then push the hell through it
to enjoy the open space

*I'm so proud of the woman you
are becoming. I see maturity
developing before my eyes,
and as my eyes water, my heart
floats.*

Snare

Matches create infernos.

Beans grow to beanstalks.

Atoms cause explosions,

and spiders eat two headed
purple snakes.

See what little things can do?

Now stop thinking I can't and
go snare your giant.

Be your own horse.
Treat yourself well,
and give yourself the ride of
your life

PERFUME

Wisps of perfumed flowers
fall upon my senses,
as if trying to saturate my
suffering with sandalwood
rain and sprinkles of musk,
or maybe just to awaken the
joy within reach.

*Scattered petals
each a suffering soul
Set adrift by someone who cast
their exquisiteness aside*

*They say there is strength in
numbers, but sometimes true
grit is found in the courage to
remove ourselves from the pack*

RIPPLE EFFECT

Ripples of emotion

keep extending out

Far reaching or surpassing

The edges of our doubt

Yes, were all connected

by an energetic fields

You exhale your atoms

then I inhale your yield

Kindness, love, compassion

will reach another soul

If you toss it in the force field

and watch the ripples go.....

Be Yourself

Have you ever seen a sunrise
from another point of view?

Looking from above it makes
it seem a bit askew,

But I've never seen such
beauty
In all my waking days

I think there is a lesson here,
to look for different ways:

To appreciate variance

To seek new ways of
understanding

To love what's in front of us,
(even if there is a ring in her
nose)

To celebrate uniqueness

CARRY ON

Do you think today is endless
when tomorrow never
comes?

And yesterday is way too late
to make it right again?

Don't be fooled by night's
dark cast, the pall that coats
your world,

It's within you, my child, the
strength to change
the hope to carry on.

*Never be so serious that
you can't sometimes laugh at
yourself*

STORIES

Some unwritten,
Some written then burned,
Some written then torn and
stomped on,
Some written the sold out on,
Some written then rewritten,
Some written then killed,
Some written then blemished,
Some not even pondered,
not even born,
Stories
Our stories
Your stories
Which one are you?
Yours, my dear, is a bit of
them all, but the final chapter
is awaiting your lead.

RAVE

Shall we spread our wings to
dance semi naked in the vast
field of loneliness?
Show our vulnerability while
gaining strength?
I say we shall.
For in time, others will join
us, and we will realize we all
crave acceptance, that we
are not alone. And soon our
vulnerable solo dance will
turn into a rave.

What storm awaits you today?
You DO have the strength to go
through it.

NE'ER

Ne'er was there ever a star so
bright,
rising over amber fields and
lush greens.
No.
Ne'er was there ever a star so
damn beautiful, filling the sky
with hopes and dreams and
cotton candy wishes.

Sigh, I'm smiling.

Ne'er was there ever a day
that I felt
such spectacular sparklets of
happiness creeping back into
my soul,

for you girl, are finally
seeking the sun

FERTILIZE

Take your ideas child,

and give them wings,

and whilst flying,

sprinkle a bit of your blood,
sweat and tears on others

so your perspiration will grow
inspiration

and fertilize a garden of
eager minded seedlings.

*For those who love deeply have
hearts that bleed profusely.
Those who don't love needn't
bother with band aids.*

BIBLE

Genesis, Exodus, Samuel,
Kings,

Chronicles, numbers, verses
and things.

A challenge by my daughter
to write about God,

her faith ten times mine, for
that I applaud.

I skimmed through the Bible
looking for inspiration,

but my hands were soon
soaked with uncertain
perspiration.

But I continued laboriously,
intent to finish this task,

but saw such scary words,
this is the Bible I asked?
Words like plague,
blasphemy, crucify, death,

Gave rise to alarm,
Geeze, God makes me sweat.

But continuing on with the
strength I'd been given,

gave rise to the words
unrelated to sinnen',

Compassion, salvation,
forgiveness of sins,

Maybe this God thing can
entice grins.

Hope and promises and love
everlasting,

even special oil used for
anointing,

My daughter's faithful spirit,
gifted me in a way,

that tear dropped my eye,
she and God moved me
today.

*Torrid rain pounds my skin,
reminds me that I'm alive.*

COME OUT

When feeling forsaken and
standing in shadows,
Defend your honor by
towering towards integrity
until the light of truth shines.

For within our field of vision is
beauty well within reach.
We just need to get out from
under that rock.

LEMONADE

If I took the world's lemons,
squeezed them all dry, then
added some sugar, no one
would cry,
because lemony sad things
should soon start to fade
and disappear fully from
sweet lemonade.

I love your smile
I love your soul
I love your words
I love you whole

PORTALS

If all of those corners,
of all those rough, tangled
edges of doubt continue to
stab into you,
and all those deep pockets
of poor judgment continue to
weigh you down,
just step through the portal
of strife and uncertainty that
surrounds you,
and blast off to a new world
of hope.

LIVE

Suffice it to say, that the deep
agonizing moment when
you realize all hope is gone
and the freight train that you
expect for years is finally
barreling down on you,
you give up.

Whistles shout, anxiety
climaxes, souls stir in a
horrible, "I'm dead way," and
the echo of the churning
of the wheels is so all
consuming that your brain
atoms worry that they will
burst from the negative
energy reeling full force
inside them.

And then life stops...

Just for a moment....

Wheels cease, whistle quiets,
anxiety disappears.
Why?
Don't know;
but maybe because
somewhere in all that
nightmarish shit,
you have a spark of hope
that says......live.

*Pacifying peace will come when
you allow that restless mind to
slumber and let love settle in.*

HEAL

A hardened soul will repel
anything tossed at it:
words,
love,
compassion,
even darts.
A stoic shell grown of misery
and trial needs two loving
hands to massage and hold,
soften and bend,
to dissolve that poisonous
and unyielding force held
protectively dear.
Hold still, beautiful one,
and allow me to reach within
to touch and let the healing
begin.

Broken Love

Yes, my child, broken love
hurts in all the nooks and
crannies, places previously
unknown to the human soul.
Each ripped shred of hope
backpacking home to its
place of residence before the
coffee sip smiles
and tentative kisses,
pounding crusty footsteps
deep and pulverizing into the
most tender recesses of a
once buoyant heart, now dark
with despair, now covered
forcefully with memory's
forlorn quilt.

But I'm so happy you can
once again feel.

SPEARS AND PETALS

And yes, life is damn hard
Every twist thrusts thorns,
Every turn spears swords,
But even as your feet bleed
crimson and the tears roll
down your sweet freckled
face, remember you also
walk amongst the petals of
daffodils
And the lone howl of love's
faithful song will keep you
company as it echoes in the
midnight gloom.

Sing along, my sweet

Shoes

So many shoes to pick, which
will you choose?

The time worn leather of the
wise grandfather?

The pointy- feet ballerina
slippers to glide and sway
and twirl across the silken
stage?

Or perhaps you'll pick the
clunky metal toe hard-hat
shoe, to keep your fancy feet
safe from unseen danger.

Or the Keds to play in, the
Jordans to jump in,
the fluffy slippers to hang on
the well worn couch.

Which shoes will you wear?
You've those choices now.
Simple,
but representing life.

LAYERS

I was in our first home years
ago peeling layers off the
wall.
Layer
After
Layer
After
Layer
After
Layer
What I found beneath was
beautiful, a testimony to a
bygone time, a simpler life,
a time where painted flower
wallpaper was art, and
people sat on the porch to
talk whilst looking each other
in the eye. There was depth
to the conversation because
it was about life, not iphones
or schedules or video games.
Fast forward a hundred years.
I do see layers today- on
onions, on children bundled
up in the cold, on cakes.
But I don't see depth, beauty
perhaps, but not depth. But
you my child have surprised
me. You've allowed me to
peel off your layers slowly
to discover things about you
that were hidden treasures,
each layer revealed a bit

more of a soul so deep I still
haven't seen its end. You are
full of promising layers, all
treasures to be discovered,
all layers that hold more then
I could possibly hold.

*And as you write your new
chapter and wander with
scholars, may God hold your
hand and lead you to the right
classroom.*

BLOOM

Did you ever see a wilted
flower?
Think of the joy and the
beauty it brought the first
time it was alive and vibrant:
the smell,
the colors,
the joy,
the peace.
That's you, sweet child. You
are my flower, but there is no
reason to wilt.
I am sorry if I neglected to
water you.
I'm sorry if I didn't feed your
soul. You are what brings
color to my life, and I promise
to nourish you every day.
I am just a beginning
gardener, but I want to tend
to you and watch you bloom.

KNOCK ME OUT

Thump, thump
Sharp bricks falling
Boom, boom,
Hit me again
Down on knees
Prayers unanswered
Ha, ha
Taunt me instead

Icons shatter, the false gods
haunt,
Hopes and dreams dive fast
Edges strike me sharply now
Knock me out at last

Brick and mortar raining
down
The tremors moving quick
Temple of doom collapses on
me
Vomit wakes me warm and
thick

Then enter sunshine,
strength, and trust
The tools of love to build,
My vomit dries, cathedral
rises, with happiness it's
filled.

Shelters me from stormy
night; it feeds my empty shell.
My new safe haven holds me

tight,
My sanctuary from hell.

*May the morning sun greet you
kindly
May the gentle breeze rustle
your hair
May the beauty of the day allow
you to breathe
May you appreciate the gifts
right in front of you*

SONG

Chirping birds fill the air this
Sunday
Their sweet hymn of devotion
mesmerizes me
So alive in song
They can only be crooning
about you
Their joy lifting my spirits,
now I'm singing too.

Dusk veiled in black,
sun takes a back seat
heading to her own funeral
where night will officiate.
May she be resurrected
tomorrow

VULTURES

And on my walk...

Amidst the kettles of vultures,
two eyes watch,
flocks soak up vitamin D,
tanning wings, committees
form on rooftops to discuss
today's gourmet decay.
Mating dances,
preying waltzes,
offer music to a mortal's
morning bath.
Carry on, on carrion, Mr.
Vulture.
Carry on indeed.
And thank you for my bird's
eye view,
a humble first for me.

TILTED

Today is better, a sunny day
blossoming after my heart
had been a tilt a whirl,
spinning out of control,
threatening to spill me onto
the filthy pavement,
leaving open wounds, inviting
more infected thoughts to
invade my fragile being.
I asked God to stop the ride.
It did stop.
And today is beautiful.

*I allow calm waters to carry me
to horizon's unknown, passing
rainbows and sunsets as I go.
I bask in the delight of earthly
surprises and find joy in the
waters below.*

THE HEALING
COVER

Comfy cozy covers are a

nice place to hide

From life

From pain

From stress

From hopelessness

Mmmmmmm

It's lovely under here.

But I smell coffee,

inhale the aroma hard.

And I'm going to drink

it too.

So I place my feet on the

floor and move.

So there comfy, cozy

covers!

Take that!

*I bequeath thee to
someone else who needs
a break. Give them respite
please.
I'm getting on with my life.*

*When feeling forsaken and
standing in shadows, defend
your honor by towering toward
integrity until the light of truth
shines.*

Travel is my Peace

Memories hit of majestic
mountains and moonlit
passages illuminating holy
shrines.
Oh, the beauty!
The tastes of potent reds in
vineyards under verandas,
Gaudi inspired perplexities, a
whimsical visionary enjoyed
with seafood paella and wine.
My heart bleeds for more!
Bejeweled shafts of light
beckon again from imposing
cathedrals of stone. I'm
coming soon! Sumptuous
colors of busy bazaars offer
the strange, the lovely, and
the, "I'll never, ever, taste
that."
My need to be a gypsy
with holes in my shoes and
wonder in my gaze, does
not coexist with my need for
simplicity, a homey sanctuary,
a thatched roof cottage,
simple, with a Guinness on
the table and a sheep in the
yard. Maybe it's merely a
function of my dysfunction, or
maybe it's just me.

MOTHER

Written by another daughter,
my Molly

To my mother
With eyes like river water
Hair like flames
Dark dotted stars on her
porcelain skin
Who has walked the realms
of hell
Watching her daughter run
with the devil
Witnessing eternal love in
marriage
Burn to ashen flames before
her
To my mother
who locks away her scars
In a chest no one has found
Or will ever find
Because she safeguards it
with smiles
And endless compassion
Hairspray and lipstick, small
talk and housework,
To my mother
whose words are soothing
water
On many foreign wounded
hearts
Who speaks casualties
through her lips
Then writes down the
universe with her pen

To my mother
who has felt the words in the
wind
Secrets in the soil
Concepts in the treetops
Sculpting them into poems
that have rippled hearts
Across the sea
To my mother
who will never know her own
worth
Under her lemon juice
stained skin
finger pinched stomach
Mascaraed eyes
Who speaks beauty
Who is beauty
For she is God's perfect
image
A creation a billion years in
the making until it was her
time
To be sent to the universe
To change my world forever
Who continues to change the
world
Sending words into the
universe
Words responsible for the sun
That beams on my cold face
Wind on my heated back
Moss under my aching feet
To my mother
who is loved more than she
knows

Or will ever know
Because she is beautiful
She is a masterpiece

COLORS

Another by the masterful Molly

All of the colors I see in the
wind
That paint the treetops and
jagged cliffs
Were formed from a woman
With skin of Maplewood
And I have learned much
about home
Finding and losing it
In the illusion of a journey
About shifting phases
Shifting people
Shifting time to make me
grow older
And when I have
I realized
That love has a limit
Bone bound in some people
That love cannot be written in
sparking jump ropes or little
queens,
But can live in the wings of a
butterfly
Every movement of its wing
propelling handcrafted
molecules into the air
Like a dance
It moves on
Like life
Like the scars of time
And the surrounding
protective tissue it learns to

grow
Like remembering the
rippling waters
Of a village kingdom where
wood skin used to flourish
Realizing that time was wrong
The past is incorrect
Only the present bares truth
So take a walk in a pebbled
pond
Seek heaven not on its
reflective surface
But on the muddy bottom
Where many things that have
died now live

A daughter is a gift
A daughter with compassion is a
rare gift
A daughter who survived a
rough journey due to another
Is one in a million
And still, you smile

COLD

Another by my Molly

I know you're cold
I know your heart has been
frosted with ice
I know your smiles are old
ones, from years ago
They froze on your face when
the snow came in
And slaughtered the warmth
I know you've searched for
love
Only to visit its grave days
later, icicles suspended at its
stone sides
I've seen you shed tears of
ice
Seen the cold winds born
from your laughter
Felt the shivering of your
broken lungs
You have braved the
snowstorm
And it has passed above our
heads
But still resides within you
So just remember
When you feel your toes and
fingers go numb
That I am thinking fondly of
you
That I wish only sunshine
upon your pale face
Blooming daisies in your

smile
Birdsong in our heart
For you were molded by a
million meadows
That cast away glaciers
And I will cast the cold away
too
If you allow me
Because I love you

HUMANITY

I believe in the brotherhood
And sisterhood of humanity
Humanhood, I'd call it
I crave it
Dearly
Where all races
All creeds
All religions
All sexes
All sexual orientations
All humanity
Come together as one
Unfortunately, that's not what
I see today.
I see
too many people fighting
their agendas
Based on race
Based on religion
Too many people with
blinders on ignoring the truth
because it doesn't fit their
purpose
Too many fools profiting from
racial crime
Ignoring their own killing their
own
or one religion killing another
Or one sex enslaved and
hidden from sight
I love God's human garden
Beauty in all its possibilities
But sometimes I wish we

were all green and talked the
same and believed the same
and were programmed the
same
For just one day
So those that believe that
"brotherhood" or "sisterhood"
is of only their choosing...
Their race better
Their sex better
Their ideas better... would be
bored as hell,
twiddling their thumbs from
the madness of a sea of puke
green
The one way conversations
The sexlessness
The roboticness
The boredom
A dull landscape of Stepford
humans
Soon they'd be begging for a
change
But,
no one would profit
Monetarily
Egotarily
Controlitarily
Sexually
from exploiting another
different
I wish some ugly hearted
people would cut the bullshit.
And return to grace,
To humanhood

We all crave acceptance
We all bleed red
Give your neighbor a hug
Find out his differences and
discover his similarities
And be thankful
You're not both green
And smile because you are
part of God's intricate garden
And he picked you to
decorate a special part of it.

*True creativity allows one artist's
view to be seen differently
through the eyes of another,
both beautiful, both true*

Death to the Inquisitor

No more must I be the
inquisitor,
the parental intelligentsia
scooping up top secret
information by way of three
party phone calls and
Facebook searches.
No more must I be the one
with a mommy warrant,
searching for whatever drug
paraphernalia you've exiled.
No more must I be the
symbolic exorciser, an evil
shooing priest purging you
of whatever devil lies within.
No more must I worry, though
of course I still do, but still,
no more must I cry myself to
sleep, blanketed by my own
frightful shivers.
I can breathe.
Finally, no more.

16 Hours

For 16 hours you've been up...
in a good way, bopping your
blonde head around college
classrooms and workplaces.

For 16 hours you've been
interacting with the world,
absorbing knowledge,
offering your wonderful gifts
to clients and friends.

For 16 hours you've lived your
exhausting life fully.

Remember when 16 hours
was hell?

I do.
But no more,
because you are
stronger than Lucifer.

THE SON

*And meanwhile as I try to parent
my other kids...*

Today I told him that love
hurts like hell,
can twist a gut into shapes
not known possible.

I heard him cry yesterday for
the first time in years,
heart wrenching, stomach
spasming sobs.

Hours later he came to me.

"Mom, what can I do to
change, to show her I'll grow
up, respect her, and be a real
man?"

FIRST KISS

And my daughter....

Giddy laugh trembles
excitedly,
dancing in the light,
refreshing air,
surrounding a budding young
woman's blushing glow.
Breaths of fresh tomorrows
skip rope on hopeful dreams.
Her first kiss didn't
disappoint.
The sparkle in her eyes said
it all.
She found a piece of heaven
whilst alive, at least for a
moment.
And she smiles,
oh how she smiles.

ANGEL

I felt the feathered touch of
silken hands,
the whispered comfort of a
beautiful woman in white, the
envelopment of my soul...that
awful day.
I imagined her wings
fluttering softly as she
lifted me after a miserable
attempt to pray, when
hope's uncertain burden
crushed me to blubbering
pulp. Somehow, still, I felt
something beautiful, and
my tears stopped as hope
changed from burden to
dream, and the goodness of a
mysterious unknown granted
me a day of peace, a glimmer
of faith's shining light.

GARDEN

God built a garden
Or somehow a garden was
built
A cosmic collision from
nothing
Or a spiritual construction
I don't care how it was born
But it's beautiful
These colors and flavors of
humanity
Meant to be cherished,
discovered,
shared, and loved.
And a few jackass advocates
for the devil
won't bring down the strong,
the united,
the high moral character of
the masses.
God bless our children and
the communities that raise
them together.

LONELY CHILD

Outside the crickets sing a
beautiful song,
more welcome than
the thunderous rains of
yesterday.
And somewhere a child lies
on a bed, a sofa, a chair,
not knowing his worth, feeling
forlorn and alone,
shades of doubt and distress
scratching his heart.
"Do I matter?" he wonders.
And a spider spins its silky
web under waning moon, as
a tired Black Lab scratches a
linoleum floor.
And not far away, though
millions of miles, another
lonely soul hugs a beat up
pillow, hoping, praying, for a
friend.

Reach out and touch a sad life

TOMORROW

When tomorrow comes:

I promise to extinguish your
fears with love's grace.

I promise to allow your hair
to tickle my nose as you
rest your tired head on my
shoulder.

I promise to nourish your
needy soul with freely gifted
compassion.

I promise to love you *just as
you are.*

SEEKING

And does the water's edge
hold love's propensity?
Yes, dear one.
Harmonious secrets wash
up and glisten within molten
sand,
held by Mother Nature's
grace,
then gifted absolution back
to watery hearth- God's
psalm,
man's cherishment, life's
shape shifting hope,
love...
adrift and alive, seeking....
seeking

ALIEN LOVE

There are hearts that beat
only to make it through
life, a quiet lazy song
accompanying human sloth.
Then there are those that fill
the chest of their owners.
I see them every day: the
givers, energetic souls
lost in their selfless
unimportance.
They paint the masterpieces
of human kindness,
colorful life canvasses
auctioned off freely to lift a
desperate soul.
Then there are those hearts
that can't contain their own
worth, like yours,
because their worth is
unknown even to themselves.
Extraordinary goodness
bleeds and bubbles over,
then eventually rises to join
atmospheric nothingness,
saturating it with the same
love gifted others, and
as it lifts beyond infinity,
I can't help but think that
light years away, a crippled
misunderstood being is being
healed from the misty risen
goodness
of you.

TELL HER

Every moment
we are reminded that we are
not promised the precious
rays of day break.
So today, tell her she's
beautiful.
Today, tell him you love him.
Today, do something exciting
for yourself. And as the sun
continues to rise,
warm the earth,
and set,
we can bet life goes on. And
if unfortunately we cease to
exist in this life, at least we
know we died trying to live.

DISCOMBOBULATED

I don't like feeling lost,
discombobulated, unsure.
As life would have it,
I do.
But if the straightest lane had
been laid out before me,
and I decided to skip down its
clear and concise path,
I wouldn't have gained the
strength needed to love you.
I wouldn't have felt the
rousing stab of unexpected
thorns, wouldn't have smelled
the disturbing pungency of
defeat,
wouldn't have risen stronger,
resolute.
Life is not about the easy
path. It's about the razor
sharp, disquieting moments
that make you bleed.
It's about the bandages that
make you heal.
It's about the scabs that
make you durable.
For only from those inelegant
gifts,
do we really appreciate the
occasional rose.

MASK

I know who you are
Under there
The barbed mask you
wear can't hide it; the truth
that's been drowned by
experience's devastating
executioner. But I still know
who you are.
You see? Look there.
Those bubbles that surface
from your drowning are the
colors of truth's rainbow,
alive with promise; and your
soulful eyes still shine with
hope in the face of adversity's
hangman.
And even when you feel like
the crushed bone dinner of
the devil himself, you fight,
and I see strength and beauty
filter up through the choking
black, a faith restoring lava,
covering, covering, covering
the sad, depressing, and
fearful until they're buried
beneath the glow of the
gladiator within.
For no one, NO ONE should
get you down.
Because you are beautiful;
you are strong; you are
thankfully unique, and you
are a gift to those who love
you,

and I know who you are

And today hope is born
Conceived of joy
and the promise of light
Bury its woeful afterbirth,
for horizon calls to guide you
forth

This flow of salty fluid echoes
with hollow emptiness
Yet the corners of my eyes
overflow, filled beyond capacity.

FEEL IT

Have you ever been really
scared?

Cry out in the night, bite
down on your tongue scared?

Lost and alone, mixed up in
your head scared?

Where is he, what is he doing
scared?

Is she alive, hurt, or in trouble
scared?

How can I possibly get
through one more day
scared?

I have,
you have,
we all have,
they all have...
been scared.

And it's cotton picken' lousy.
Miserable.
Horrible.
Soul searing.
Rip roaring bad.
Feel it.

It's ok.
You're strong. It's ok
It's ok.
It is ok

SPACE

You asked me about space in
a way I hadn't thought.
I expected to try to turn
Copernicus on his head or
throw Galileo through a black
hole.
I'd thought I'd stretch my
mind to the farthest limits
of the unknown, hoping
for a revelation, a peek
into understanding the not
understandable, fighting brain
straining implosion as I found
some sort of awareness to
a perfectly placed puzzle,
bound by a limitless, ever-
changing frame.
But you ask of space
between people and what to
fill it with. Don't you already
know the answer to that?
Love, sweet child, the answer
is simply love

*Love is the ultimate medicine,
better than cod liver oil. By far.
Take a few teaspoons.*

PETAL

If I were to place a petal in
your hand, would you release
it in the wind to fly on soft air?

Or would you carry it tenderly
between the soft round of
your thumb and the tender
caress of your palm?

Would you press it gently
between Dickens and
Whitman to dry with
memories we have shared?

Or would you set it atop a
shelf to be seen, a reminder
of our relationship, our
beauty?

What would you do with it,
love? You see, I've planted a
garden of hope with seeds
of your grace, and it is you,
my dear, who will gift me a
thousand blossoms.

One tender petal, one soft
silken fragile bit, will forever
hold the richest treasure
imaginable. A little bit of us.

BARNES AND NOBLE

And on the home front...

Her disquiet unnerves me,
throws me back to another
daughter and her hell.
Leathery hands, slick oil
sweat drape her face, sick
puppy pants, she needs to
get out.
Now.
"I'm going crazy," she
murmurs.
I contemplate doctors,
psychiatrists,
anything to calm her nerves.
But instead she guides me to
the solution.
Five bucks and a lift to Barnes
and Noble, where she sits
and writes day in and day out,
a masterpiece forming under
the deft fingers of a 16 year
old panic stricken genius.
I gladly pay for her lattes.
It's a hell of a lot cheaper
than therapy, and it returns
me with a huge teenage
smile.

FACES WITH NAMES

There are faces
behind the disease. Loved
faces.
Faces with names like Justin,
Michael, Debbie, Josh.
Beautiful faces once filled
with hope and promise and a
wide open future.
Faces loved by their parents,
their kids,
their friends.
Dark faces.
Light faces.
Long faces.
Round faces.
Faces created from love,
then cherished and groomed
and guided and kissed.
Faces who did what all of
us have done at one time or
another.
Made a mistake.
Faces who have felt like we
have.
Insecure.
Not good enough.
Scared.
Sad.
Overwhelmed.
Human faces.
Imperfect faces.
Faces representing every
damn child in America.

Beautiful faces faced with
hard choices.
To fit in.
To look cool.
To erase pain.
Faces attached to good
hearts,
Giving faces
Faces who didn't know their
susceptibility to a substance
greater than their will.
Faces that didn't know they'd
soon be under an evil spell.
Faces that couldn't fight
anymore.
Faces that left their loved
ones with just memories.
Faces that now represent a
fight to save other faces who
too are struggling,
who too have loving families,
who too didn't know the
power of the devil, who too
have hope to live.
Thank you Justin, Michael,
Debbie, and Josh for gracing
us with your lives and for
starting a deeply needed
conversation.
Your faces
Your souls
Your spirits
Your grace
will never be forgotten.

REMOTE

I press on the bruised
skin of the remote, hoping
for relief, a trip to Mars
or the dusty wilds of the
pyramids, perhaps a stomp
around a climatic mystery
would do; but I'm still here,
sitting on stained cushions,
tiptoeing around my mind's
magnanimous seesaw of
doubt, waiting for a call from
the straight A student softball
pitcher who once danced
an Irish jig for her class and
hugged me close before
bedtime. I fiddle with the
remote half crazed with hope,
half dead with despair, and
I ask myself over and over,
"Have I saved you?"
Then the call comes,
"Hi, Mom. School was great
today, I got an A."
And I remember that I didn't
save you. I know now that
you have saved yourself.

OPTIMISM

Maybe I will forget the past.
Maybe time's cold hand
will do its job, shaking each
screaming moment, each
violent episode, from my
memory;
pushing,
shoving,
each drug fueled snapshot
over the edge of my
remembrance until they all
come tumbling down,
free flying in midair, smashing,
shattering,
flinging,
all the old crap into oblivion's
eternal heaven.
Yes, maybe I will forget. And
your recovery and optimism
is allowing me the hope that
I will.

TRUTH

Truth.

Can hurt like hell.

Truth.

Can liberate.

Truth.

Can bring out a brave
side.

Truth.

Can destroy.

Truth.

Can cause reconsideration.

Truth.

Can make us look inward.

Truth.

Can make us look outward.

It's real.

It's honest.

It's naked.

It's harsh.

It's direct

It's true.

AND IT HEALS.

Don't be afraid of your own
truth.

You'd be surprised at the
support you'll receive when
the disguise come off.

SMOKE

The soft tendrils of smoke
pirouette in the air, a cancer
laced dance, breaking their
performance by taking refuge
in my throat as they dig their
sharp toes into the tender red
flesh inside.
I'm choking, drowning in
a sea of hazy Marlboro
emissions,
and I feel a disease begin,
waltzing with the skanky,
sooty, reeking skirt and
sweater I now wear.
But I must accept,
must sit with the cryptic fog
in a dark room, must keep
quiet as my breath becomes
shallow and my head
becomes light.
After all, I am the mom and
I've come here to learn.

GOODBYE POISON

The toxicity has left.
The spiraling thunderbolts of
electric madness have quietly
and quickly gone away. One
day it became clear again,
and the sun burst through the
clouds like a ripped football
banner. One day the world
began again and the clock
started to move forward,
seconds, minutes, hours. I
noticed at the same time how
the moistened petals of the
rose opened and gleamed,
how the birds sang songs
of indescribable sweetness,
how a baby's cry became
music to my ears. The day the
toxicity left, I started to live.
The day it left we started a
new journey together.

SKIPPING STONES

Heaven must be a step below
this. It has to be. For nowhere
else could I feel such intense
joy and see such deep
beauty. The rippling waters
of the Delaware lap my bare
feet as the old ship sails
on by. I'm here seeing this,
listening to the gulls, skipping
stones with my youngest
child, smelling the luxurious
aroma of seaweed and a bit
of trash. But it's better than
heaven, because somewhere
you decided to live and
somewhere far away on
Earth's water's edge, you are
skipping stones too.

GATE

There upon the rusted
swinging gate sits a
redheaded child, her face
sprinkled with the kisses of
angels. Her torn sneaker digs
into a rusted bar, a viable
hope for stability. I watch
her unknowing face, still
innocent and unaware of the
challenges she will face only
a few years from now. She
jumps off, snagging her dress,
tearing it away without a care
in the world. As she skips
happily towards the lake, the
fresh smell of daisies pierces
my nostrils. I breathe it in
and cherish this moment of
bliss and innocence. I don't
want that child to know
the dangers ahead of her. I
want her to keep smelling
the daisies and swinging on
rusted gates.

JUMP

The deep red of the

parachute carved a lithe

design into the pale blue

of the summer

sky's landscape.

I'd always thought them

crazy, you know the

type that risk their lives

for a thrill. Now I envy

them. After living in

life's darkest shadows, I

wish I'd the courage to

fly.

THE CHANGE

As steam escapes the
confines of its prior liquid life,

And caterpillars change their
form to butterflies in flight,

And snowy blankets melt
away to newly sodden spring,

And rage filled storms give
way to rainbows only God
can bring;

A blond haired lass once dark
as night once imprisoned and
sedated,

Changes course and seeks
the light,
Finally liberated!

LIVING

A poem by her

Do you know what peace
feels like?

Real peace?

The kind of peace when
explosive volcanic magma
turns into igneous rock?

The silence of the land when
the waters recede back into
the sea after swallowing it
whole?

Calm after destruction.

Destruction that brings you
close to death.

Yet you were already dead.
The walking dead.

Do you know what
resurrection feels like?

The pain of transforming back
into a living being?

The terrifying thoughts,
actions, feelings?

But then, the first time

noticing how blue the sky is.
The birds in the trees, the
shapes of the clouds, the
scent of a flower.

Uninhibited beauty in all its
glory.

Do you know how it feels to
love, and be loved?

The kind of love after years of
isolation?

Throwing knives and
cannonballs at anyone who
dared to even come close.

To opening up your soul.

To caring about the hearts of
others before your own, and
feeling satisfaction and joy.

Do you know what its like to
live?

Really live?

The kind of loving after a
coma?

The relieving gasp of air after
drowning?

Taking in each moment good
and bad.

Feeling unconditional
love and sincere youthful
happiness.

Learning, growing, feeling.

Appreciating each and every
moment on this God given
earth.

Tuning out the noise of life
and taking time to appreciate
the littlest of things.

To be ever grateful.

Do you know what it's like to
love life?

To feel free?

I do.

And I know you can too.

HORIZON

I looked over at the amber
glow of the new moon as
it shined on the glistening
asphalt. A summer rain had
fallen, and the drops of
liquid lingered, sparkling,
a reminder that jewels live
here, in this very house. I
know you're over there now,
many miles away, a wise
decision, given the relapse
rate of returning addicts. As
much as I miss you, I know
you are better there, will
carve out a beautiful life. I
know that you have risen,
as the sun above a dreary
landscape, a moon above a
dark wooded path. You have
indeed risen, so I name this
book for your resurrection
my dear, so proud of your
rising.

My Words

About the Author

Maureen Fitzpatrick is a former teacher and a mother of five. She enjoys travel, reading, and community service. She wants you to know that you are not alone.